EXPLORING SCIENCE

Teaching Units, Exploration Centers, Activities And Ideas For Primary Grades

by
Imogene Forte & Sandra Schurr

Incentive Publications, Inc.
Nashville, Tennessee

Illustrated by Gayle Seaberg Harvey
Cover by Maribeth Wright
Edited by Sally Sharpe

ISBN 0-86530-014-3

Table Of Contents

HOW TO USE THIS BOOK

EXPLORING SCIENCE provides primary teachers with carefully developed skills-based plans and procedures for presenting creative and stimulating science activities in the areas of earth, life and physical science. The topical units in this book have been created in keeping with Bloom's taxonomy of cognitive development in order to stimulate varied thinking skills as well as teach basic science concepts. Every unit contains a student-ready, reproducible activity for each of the six stages of learning: knowledge, comprehension, application, analysis, synthesis, and evaluation.

In addition to the activities, each unit includes a teacher overview page which outlines the learning concepts and lists the activities, materials needed and any other enrichment and extension ideas and projects. All of the units have one or two "learning bonus" pages which contain suggested vocabulary listings, bulletin board ideas, and creative activities. Ten of the units also have a student-ready, reproducible "just for fun" page which offers a puzzle, hidden picture or other fun activity for stimulating students' interest. What's more, six exploration centers have been included to diversify and enrich your science program. Each exploration unit plan shows you how to set up the center, tells you what materials you will need, and gives you 18 exploration challenges which are ready to reproduce, cut apart and use. These challenges may be mounted on 5" x 7" cards and placed in the center for individual or small group use or distributed as complete sets to students for use as task cards.

But that's not all! A "Super-useful Appendix" contains handy reproducibles including a topical overview, a student profile work sheet, a reference guide for developing primary units and activities, ideas for "smuggling" science into the classroom, and a listing of free and inexpensive materials complete with suggestions for their use in science centers. All of the units and exploration centers have been grouped according to their respective science areas for your convenience. Moreover, a complete index allows you to quickly and easily locate specific topics or items.

This primary science resource will enable you to extend science concepts, reinforce skill development, and encourage students to explore the world around them!

ROCKS

UNIT AT A GLANCE

CONCEPT CAPSULE

Children will . . .
- understand that natural forces change the shape, appearance, and make up of rocks
- understand that rocks have different characteristics and may be identified and grouped according to these characteristics
- become familiar with the physical properties of various rocks
- understand the definitions of vocabulary words pertaining to the study of rocks and be able to apply these words as they learn about rocks

MATERIALS NEEDED

pencils, crayons and/or markers, hand lenses, masking tape, rock collection (12 or more rocks), paint, buttons, small pebbles, ribbon or felt

ACTIVITIES

Knowledge: Rock Hunt
scavenger hunt activity

Comprehension: Describe A Rock
observation work sheet

Application: Rock Predictions
drawing/writing activity

Analysis: Examining A Rock
observation/experimentation work sheet

Synthesis: Words About Rocks
word find activity

Evaluation: If I Were A Rock . . .
drawing activity

LEARNING BONUS

Vocabulary
Collector's Corner/Bulletin Board
Rock Hounds
Please Don't Pet The Pet Rocks

Evaluation Discussion:
  A Rock Is Like A History Book
Share A Rock Homework Wrist Band

JUST FOR FUN

Rocky Tales

ROCK HUNT

KNOWLEDGE

Go on a rock hunt with your class.
Find each of the rocks described below.
Put a check beside each description as you find that kind of rock.

1. A rock smaller than the fingernail on your little finger
2. A square rock
3. A very rough rock
4. A rock bigger than your fist
5. A rock with something growing on it
6. A round, smooth rock
7. A rock of more than one color
8. A rock that "makes you feel good"
9. A rock that would make a good paperweight
10. A rock that would make a nice gift for someone special
11. A rock that is very light in color or very dark in color
12. A shiny rock

DESCRIBE A ROCK

COMPREHENSION

Choose at least five rocks from the class rock collection.
Write as many descriptive words for each rock as you can.
Use the adjectives below or add your own.

Rock 1   Rock 2

_____

_____

_____

_____

_____

_____

Rock 3   Rock 4

_____

_____

_____

_____

_____

_____

Rock 5

_____

_____

_____

_____

_____

_____

Adjectives:

hard	crystal-like	dull	oblong
soft	grainy	shiny	bumpy
round	light	heavy	rough
square	dark	oval	striped

ROCK PREDICTIONS

APPLICATION

Look at each picture below.
Predict how each rock will be changed by the force written beside it.
Draw a picture of each rock's new form or write a description of it in
  the space given.

BEFORE	CHANGED BY	AFTER
	Digging Animals	
	Growing Trees	
	Harsh Winds	
	Flowing Water	
	Freezing and Melting Water	

EXAMINING A ROCK

ANALYSIS

You will need these materials:

       hand lens   masking tape
       pencil   10 rocks

1. Put a piece of masking tape on each rock.
2. Label the rocks 1 - 10.
3. Examine one rock at a time.
4. Answer these questions about each rock.
   Write your answers on the chart below.

   a. What color is the rock?
   b. Does the rock have specks?
   c. Is the rock smooth?
   d. Does the rock have stripes?
   e. Is the rock shiny?
   f. Does the rock float in water?
   g. Does the rock make marks on paper?

Rock	Color?	Specks?	Smooth?	Stripes?	Shiny?	Float?	Marks on paper?
1							
2							
3							
4							
5							
6							
7							
8							
9							
10							

WORDS ABOUT ROCKS

SYNTHESIS

Make a word find puzzle using the descriptive words you used in the
     activity "Describe A Rock" (page 11).
Add the vocabulary words for this unit if you like.
Be sure to make an answer key for your puzzle!

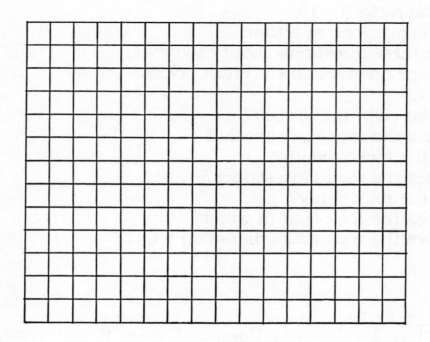

Words to find:

_____

_____

_____

_____

IF I WERE A ROCK . . .

EVALUATION

If you were a rock, what kind of rock would you like to be?
Would you rather be part of a house foundation, a rock garden,
   a stone bridge, or a gravel driveway?
Draw a picture of the kind of rock you would most like to be.
Be able to give reasons for your choice.

LEARNING BONUS

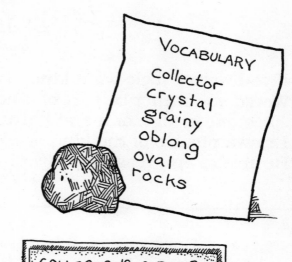

Collector's Corner/Bulletin Board

Gather pictures of various kinds of rocks and display them on the bulletin board. Arrange the completed "Words About Rocks" word find puzzles (synthesis activity) around the rock pictures. Cut letters out of construction paper to spell "Collector's Corner" for the caption. Place a table near the bulletin board containing the class rock collection. Have students contribute to the collection if you like. Ask students to find pictures of other rocks to add to the bulletin board and to bring new rocks to add to the class collection.

Rock Hounds

Encourage students to become rock hounds by searching for rocks of all shapes, sizes, colors and textures. Instruct the students to classify their rocks according to each characteristic respectively: shape, size, color and texture. Then have students rank order the rocks using these criteria:

- lightest to heaviest
- dullest to shiniest
- least colorful to most colorful
- smoothest to roughest

Please Don't Pet The Pet Rocks

Have each student select a special rock to make into a pet. Let the students make their pet rocks come alive by decorating them with paint, ribbon or felt, buttons and small pebbles. Plan and construct a classroom pet rock zoo by making signs, cages and scenery. Ask each student to write a "How To Take Care Of A Pet Rock" booklet for his or her pet rock.

Evaluation Discussion: A Rock Is Like A History Book

Discuss with the class how a rock is like a history book. Stimulate the discussion by asking questions such as "How have scientists learned about the past through the study of rocks?" Ask students what kinds of things rocks tell us and how this information may be used to uncover mysteries. Encourage the students to think of new ways that rocks might be of use in learning about the past and providing helpful knowledge for shaping the future.

Share A Rock Homework Wrist Band

Ask each student to select a rock from his or her own rock collection to carry home in his or her pocket. Instruct the students to use the vocabulary and the classification criteria from this unit to share their rocks with family members. Have each student cut out a wrist band and write the following on it:

inside - I'd like to tell you two things about this rock -- where I found it and how I think it got there.

outside - Ask me about the rock in my pocket.

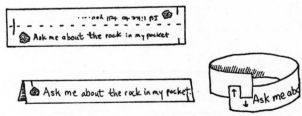

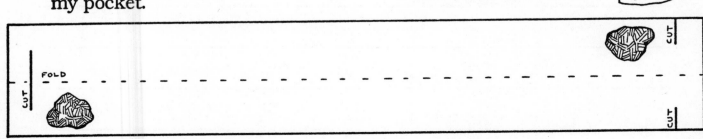

ROCKY TALES

JUST FOR FUN

Select one of the "rocky story starters" below.
Use the story starter to write a tall tale.

The sign read "beware of falling rocks," but the driver drove straight ahead until . . .

The class had just finished making pet rocks and had placed the "pets" in a row on the windowsill when . . .

Right before my eyes the tiny little rock began to get bigger, and bigger, and bigger . . .

_____
(title)

_____

_____

_____

_____

_____

_____

_____

SEASONS AND WEATHER

UNIT AT A GLANCE

CONCEPT CAPSULE

Children will . . .
- identify seasons of the year and the weather characteristic of each
- recognize the changes in nature that occur during each season
- associate symbols with types of weather
- become familiar with the weather tendencies in specific geographical locations
- realize that certain places in the US have very little change in climate throughout the year

MATERIALS NEEDED

pencils, scissors, paste, crayons, construction paper, straight pins

ACTIVITIES

Knowledge: Four Seasons
identification work sheet

Comprehension: Branches For Every Season
cut and paste work sheet

Application: Be A Weather Forecaster
drawing activity

Analysis: Picture Predictions
association work sheet

Synthesis: Seasonal Designs
drawing activity

Evaluation: Summer All Year Long!
observation, questions and answers work sheet

LEARNING BONUS

Vocabulary
Weather Bulletin/Bulletin Board
What If . . .

FOUR SEASONS

KNOWLEDGE

Spring, summer, winter and fall are the four seasons of the year.
Write the name of the correct season for each picture below.
Color the pictures.

BRANCHES FOR EVERY SEASON

COMPREHENSION

Cut out the tree branches below.
Paste each branch on the tree in the correct seasonal picture.

BE A WEATHER FORECASTER

APPLICATION

Invent a symbol to show what the weather
is like where you live for each day of
this school week.

Monday	
Tuesday	
Wednesday	
Thursday	
Friday	

PICTURE PREDICTIONS

ANALYSIS

Study the weather symbols on the calendars below.
Decide what season is shown by the symbols on each
calendar and write the *season* name at the top of the
calendar.

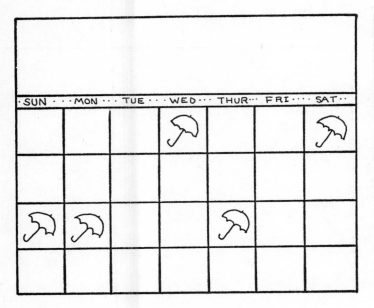

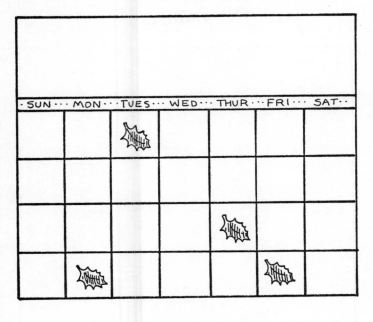

SEASONAL DESIGNS

SYNTHESIS

Use your imagination to create a symbol with a special pattern or
   design for each of the four seasons.
Be sure to use colors that make you think of each season.
Draw the symbols below.

spring

summer

fall

winter

SUMMER ALL YEAR LONG!

EVALUATION

Some places have very limited changes in climate such as Florida and Alaska.

Look at the pictures of Florida and Alaska below and then answer the following questions.

1. Judging from what you see in the picture, what is the weather like in Alaska?
2. Judging from what you see in the picture, what is the weather like in Florida?
3. What would be most difficult for an Eskimo to adapt to when moving to Florida?
4. What would be most difficult for a Floridian to adapt to when moving to Alaska?
5. What would be most difficult for *you* to adapt to when moving to an entirely different climate?

   Where would you most prefer to live and why?

LEARNING BONUS

Weather Bulletin/Bulletin Board

Cover the bulletin board with colorful paper. Make weather symbol patterns using construction paper: a mitten for cold weather, a snowman for snowy weather, an umbrella for rainy weather, a cloud for cloudy weather, a sun for sunny weather, and a flower for hot weather. Attach the symbols to the board with straight pins. Write each day of the week on a strip of construction paper and pin them to the left side of the board. Make a large "box" in the center of the board for a weather bulletin. Attach a square of clear plastic to the bottom of the square as shown so that the daily temperature may be written and wiped off easily. Have the students listen to the weather forecast on the radio or television each night and write down the weather prediction for the next day. Each day in class, pin the appropriate weather symbols in the weather bulletin box and write the temperature. The class will enjoy "checking up on the weather forecaster" to see if he or she makes accurate predictions!

VOCABULARY
calendar
climate
forecast
nature
prediction
season
symbol
weather

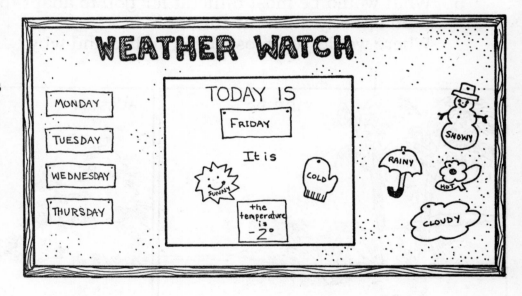

What If . . .

Have each student write a short paragraph about one of these "what if" statements.

1. What if there were never a change in the season?
2. What if each person could choose the season that he or she would like to live in for the rest of his or her life?
3. What if it never rained in the spring or never snowed in the winter?
4. What if the sun forgot to shine in the summer or the leaves forgot to fall in autumn?

ANIMALS
UNIT AT A GLANCE

CONCEPT CAPSULE
Children will . . .
- become familiar with the protective and adaptive functions of particular animal body parts
- identify the habitats of various animals
- gain an appreciation of the special needs and ways of life of particular animals
- be able to name specific animals which use camouflage for protection
- understand that animals play an important role in nature's cycle by being helpful and harmful
- recognize that certain animals have become endangered due to man's carelessness and/or harmful practices

MATERIALS NEEDED
pencils, crayons, scissors, paste, construction paper, magazines, butcher paper, markers

ACTIVITIES
Knowledge: Animal I.D.
identification work sheet

Comprehension: Animals Have Homes, Too
drawing activity

Application: If I Were An Animal . . .
investigative research work sheet

Analysis: Animals In Hiding
hidden picture activity

Synthesis: Design A Home
drawing/writing activity

Evaluation: My Scrapbook Of Very Important Animals
creative construction activity

LEARNING BONUS

Vocabulary
Mothers And Their Babies/Bulletin Board
What Animal Am I?
Animal Commodities

Evaluation Discussion:
Animals That Help And Hurt
In Search Of Animal Products
Homework Wrist Band

JUST FOR FUN
King Of The Jungle

27

ANIMAL I.D.

KNOWLEDGE

Animals have special body parts called adaptations which help them
   to get food and to protect themselves.
Below are ears, feet, and tails belonging to five different animals.
Write the name of the correct animal in each box.

1. _____

2. _____

3. _____

4. _____

5. _____

Answer Key on pages 124 and 125.

ANIMALS HAVE HOMES, TOO

COMPREHENSION

Every animal has its own habitat or place to live.
Draw the habitat for each animal below.

IF I WERE AN ANIMAL . . .

APPLICATION

Select an animal that you would like to be.
Collect information about this animal in order to answer the
  questions below.
Draw or write the answers to these questions in the space below.

What animal would you choose to be?

Where would you live?

What kind of food would you eat?

How would you hide from your enemies and how would you protect
  yourself?

Would you make a good pet?
Why or why not?

ANIMALS IN HIDING

ANALYSIS

Some animals use camouflage to hide from their enemies.
Other animals have sharp teeth or excellent eyesight to help protect
  themselves.
Examine the picture below to discover the animals hiding from their
  enemies.
Circle each animal and label it with the correct protective feature(s).
One is done for you.

sharp claws, teeth

Answer Key on pages 124 and 125.

DESIGN A HOME

SYNTHESIS

Choose an animal and design a special home for it.
Consider things such as its size, physical needs, habits, etc.
Draw your plans and sketches below.
List reasons for designing the home as you did.

MY SCRAPBOOK OF VERY IMPORTANT ANIMALS

EVALUATION

Make a scrapbook of the ten animals you consider to be most important.
Cut pictures of the animals out of magazines or draw your own portraits.
Try to include the natural habitat of each animal.
Label the pictures and bind them together in a scrapbook designed by
   you.
List your criteria for choosing each animal on this page.

Animal   Criteria

1. _____

2. _____

3. _____

4. _____

5. _____

6. _____

7. _____

8. _____

9. _____

10. _____

LEARNING BONUS

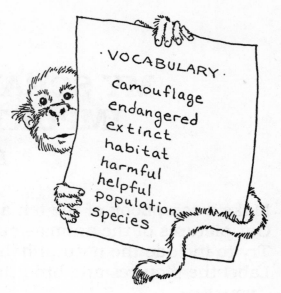

Mothers And Their Babies/Bulletin Board

Find pictures of female animals and their babies. Arrange the pictures on the bulletin board so that no pair is together. Cut letters out of construction paper for the caption "Mothers And Their Babies." Use construction paper to make a banner which says "Match the mothers and their babies" and another which says "Can you name the babies?" Change the pictures periodically as you study the unit.

MOTHERS AND THEIR BABIES

MATCH THE MOTHERS AND THEIR BABIES.

CAN YOU NAME THE BABIES ?

What Animal Am I?

Have the class play animal charades! Ask each student to choose an animal to imitate. Have the other students try to guess the animal. Emphasize the importance of representing true characteristics and habits of animals such as the way an elephant walks, the way a fish swims, the way a snake slithers, the way a kangaroo hops, etc. You participate, too, in order to build the students' enthusiasm!

34

Animal Commodities

Help the class make a large collage of animals and their products by cutting pictures out of magazines and by drawing pictures. Include such animals and products as bees and honey, cows and milk, elephants and ivory, birds and feathers, sheep and wool, etc. Provide the students with magazines, scissors, crayons, markers and any other supplies you would like. Encourage creativity. Remind the students that a collage is supposed to be unusual and colorful. Display the collage in the classroom for all to see.

Evaluation Discussion: Animals That Help And Hurt

Discuss with students ways that animals are both helpful and harmful to man. Then discuss ways that man has been helpful or harmful to animals. Lead into a discussion of endangered species such as the eagle, seal and wolverine. Have each student prepare a speech to present to the class about an endangered species.

In Search Of Animal Products Homework Wrist Band

Have each student cut out a wrist band and write the following on it:

inside - Today I learned that animals produce many things that are useful to people.

outside - Will you help me find three things in our home that were produced by animals?

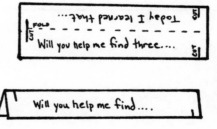

FOLD

CUT

CUT

CUT

KING OF THE JUNGLE

JUST FOR FUN

Select an animal from those below to be king of the jungle.
Circle your choice.
Design a robe and a crown for the king.
Give a good reason for your choice.

BIRDS

UNIT AT A GLANCE

CONCEPT CAPSULE
Children will . . .
- be able to identify and name the basic parts of a bird
- learn the natural habitats of various birds
- observe birds eating at homemade feeders
- become familiar with the adaptation of bird bills and feet
- gain an appreciation of the beauty of birds and their role in nature
- become aware of the eagle's endangered state

MATERIALS NEEDED
pencils, crayons and/or markers, egg cartons, string or twine, birdseed, scissors, paste, magazines, construction paper, recordings of bird calls, net sacks (for fruit, potatoes, onions, etc.)

ACTIVITIES
Knowledge: Label A Bird
diagram work sheet

Comprehension: Where Do Birds Live?
drawing activity

Application: A Bird Feeder Of Your Very Own
construction activity

Analysis: Birds Of Many Bills And Feet
observation/question-answer work sheet

Synthesis: If Birds Could Talk . . .
creative writing activity

Evaluation: All American Bird
reasoning activity

LEARNING BONUS
Vocabulary
A Little Bird Told Me/Bulletin Board
Bird Walk
Bird Calling Contest

Evaluation Discussion:
   How Are Birds Helpful?
Help A Bird In Your Own Backyard
Bird Talk

JUST FOR FUN
Birds Worth Remembering

LABEL A BIRD

KNOWLEDGE

Label the parts of the bird below.

crown   belly   back
bill   feet   throat
breast   wing   rump

_____

WHERE DO BIRDS LIVE?

COMPREHENSION

Birds live in many different places.
Draw the natural habitat for each bird as it is described below.

Red cardinals live in backyards
close to homes.

Yellow warblers live in bushy
places near streams or ponds.

Black crows live in fields and
farm lands.

Brown whippoorwills live in the
deep woods.

Blue herons live along the beach near large bodies of water.

A BIRD FEEDER
OF YOUR VERY OWN

APPLICATION

Follow the simple directions below to make your very own bird feeder.

1. Find a plastic or heavy cardboard egg carton.
2. Punch four holes in the carton as shown in the illustration.
3. Attach a long piece of string or twine to the carton as shown.
4. Hang the feeder from a branch of a tree.
5. Fill the feeder with birdseed and observe the birds that come to eat!

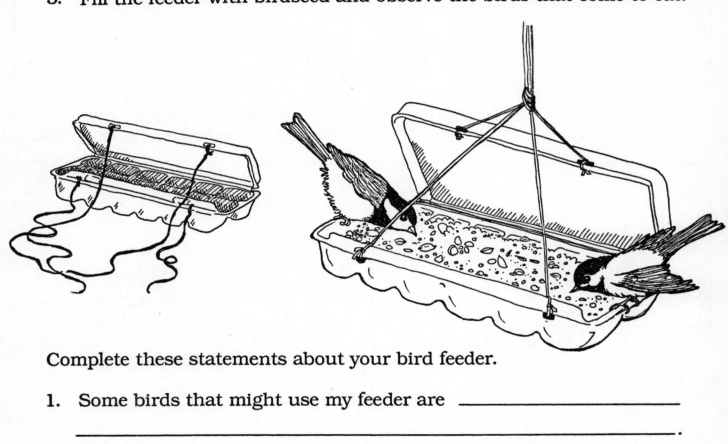

Complete these statements about your bird feeder.

1. Some birds that might use my feeder are _____
   _____.

2. Some kinds of food I can put in my feeder are _____
   _____.

3. Some places I could hang my feeder are _____
   _____.

4. Some problems I could have with my feeder are _____
   _____.

BIRDS OF MANY
BILLS AND FEET

ANALYSIS

A. Study the adaptations of the bird bills and feet below.
    Determine which bill would be best for each of these purposes.

1. _____ seed eating
2. _____ insect eating
3. _____ preying

4. _____ ground feeding
5. _____ fish eating
6. _____ probing

Determine which feet would be best for each of these purposes.

7. _____ swimming
8. _____ perching

9. _____ climbing
10. _____ preying

B. 1. Why do birds have bills and feet of different sizes and shapes?

    _____

    2. How does the food a bird eats determine the habitat in which the bird
        must live?

    _____

    3. Which types of bills and feet would be found on birds in:

    a wooded area _____

    an area near water _____

    an open field _____

Answer Key on pages 124 and 125.

IF BIRDS COULD TALK . . .

SYNTHESIS

Imagine what the world would be like if birds could talk!

What would birds say to cats?

_____

What would birds say about telephone wires?

_____

What would birds say about worms?

_____

What would birds say about bird watchers . . . like you?

_____

ALL AMERICAN BIRD

EVALUATION

The eagle, our national bird, is in danger of becoming extinct.
If this tragic possibility should occur, which of the birds below would you
   choose to represent our country -- the pelican, woodpecker, robin, owl or
   pigeon?
List your choice and reasons for that choice below.

LEARNING BONUS

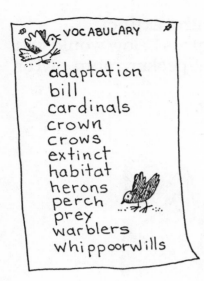

VOCABULARY

adaptation
bill
cardinals
crown
crows
extinct
habitat
herons
perch
prey
warblers
whippoorwills

A Little Bird Told Me/Bulletin Board

Provide the class with a variety of magazines. Instruct each student to find and cut out a picture of a bird in one of the magazines. Have the students write one or two paragraph stories that their selected birds might "tell." Students may write their stories on pieces of construction paper and then paste their bird pictures on them. Arrange the stories on a bulletin board with the caption "A Little Bird Told Me . . . ."

Bird Walk

Take the class on a bird walk around the school grounds or immediate neighborhood. Before leaving on the walk, discuss with the students the various kinds of homes, feeding habits, nests, eggs, etc. of birds. Ask the students to see how many birds they can spot on the walk and to try to find out as much about them as they can. After the walk, take the class to the library to research the birds they saw. Have each student gather enough information about one bird to give a brief report to the class.

Bird Calling Contest

Go to the library and check out several records or tapes of bird calls. Allow the students time to listen to the calls and to practice mimicking them. Choose a day to have a class bird calling contest. (If possible, invite a bird watcher or other bird "specialist" to judge the contest.) Award the best caller with an appropriate prize.

Evaluation Discussion: How Are Birds Helpful?

Discuss with the class how birds can be helpful to us. Encourage the students to suggest their own ideas and observations. Include in the discussion that birds help us by helping farmers keep their fields free of weeds, by eating insects that are harmful to plants, by giving us meat and eggs, and in many other ways. Ask the students to describe what the world would be like without birds.

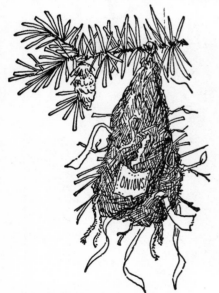

Help A Bird In Your Own Backyard

Take the class on a scavenger hunt for items that would be good for building bird nests such as lightweight twigs, straw, stalks of dried grass, rubber bands (cut apart), pieces of yarn or string, etc. Have each student make a "do-it-yourself kit" for a bird in his or her backyard by filling a net bag (fruit, onion, or potato sack) with nest building items. Let students take their bags home and tie them to a low tree branch. Students will enjoy keeping watch to see if a new nester uses the materials!

Bird Talk

Have the students write clever things that a bald eagle might say to a sparrow, a fish, a helicopter, and an American flag. Then ask each student to write a paragraph from a bird's point of view about what life would be like if a bird's beak were made of foam rubber. Display the papers on a bulletin board or in a science exploration center.

BIRDS WORTH REMEMBERING

JUST FOR FUN

Look carefully at this picture for three minutes.
Then cover the picture with a clean sheet of paper and write the names
of as many birds as you can remember on the paper.

Answer Key on pages 124 and 125.

DINOSAURS

UNIT AT A GLANCE

CONCEPT CAPSULE

Children will . . .

- be able to recognize and identify characteristics of several dinosaurs
- gain an understanding of the nature of the prehistoric world and its inhabitants
- gain an appreciation of the work of paleontologists
- become familiar with the trachodon's appearance and way of life
- recognize the immense changes that have occurred in the physical world and its inhabitants since prehistoric times

MATERIALS NEEDED

pencils, crayons, butcher paper, old socks and other scrap materials for puppets

ACTIVITIES

Knowledge: Dinosaur Decisions
matching work sheet

Comprehension: A Dinosaur's World
drawing activity

Application: Scientist At Work
completion/drawing activity

Analysis: Meet The Triceratops
following directions/drawing activity

Synthesis: My Pet Dinosaur
creative thinking activity

Evaluation: What Happened?
visual imagery activity

LEARNING BONUS

Vocabulary
Dinosaur Search/Bulletin Board
Story Starters
Puppet Parade

Evaluation Discussion:
  Why Are Dinosaurs Extinct?
Dino-mite Homework
  Wrist Band

JUST FOR FUN

Dinosaur Dot-To-Dot

DINOSAUR DECISIONS

KNOWLEDGE

Match the picture of each dinosaur with the correct description
   by writing the correct letter in each blank.
Color the dinosaurs.

1. ____ Brachiosaurus' front legs are longer than its back legs. It has a small head and a long heavy neck.

2. ____ Stegosaurus has pointed, bony plates on its back and a spiked tail for protection.

3. ____ Triceratops has a parrot-beak jaw, a three-foot horn above each eye, and a short horn on its nose.

4. ____ Tyrannosaurus has tearing claws on its three-toed feet and six-inch-long saw-toothed teeth.

5. ____ Protoceratops has a large head and a parrot-like beak.

6. ____ Iguanodon, a plant-eating dinosaur, has short thumbs which are like sharp spikes. It is approximately 15 feet high and 30 feet long.

Answer Key on pages 124 and 125.

A DINOSAUR'S WORLD

COMPREHENSION

Dinosaurs lived millions of years ago when the world was very different.
During the time in which dinosaurs lived there were only trees, plants,
rivers, fish, insects, and other dinosaurs and prehistoric creatures.
Complete the picture of the prehistoric world below by drawing the
natural environment and other prehistoric creatures.

SCIENTIST AT WORK

APPLICATION

A paleontologist is a scientist who studies dinosaur bones.
Pretend that you are a paleontologist and have just uncovered part of a
   dinosaur skeleton.
Finish the skeleton below by drawing and coloring what you think the
   dinosaur looked like.

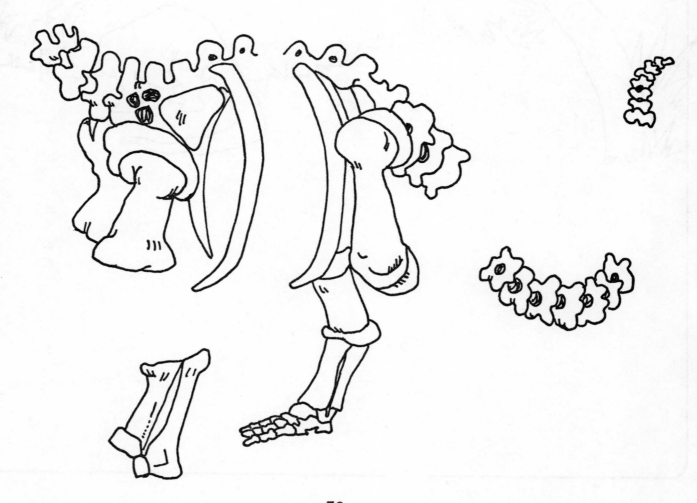

MEET THE TRICERATOPS

ANALYSIS

Study the picture of the triceratops below.
Add the missing parts by following these directions.

1. Draw a parrot-like beak.
2. Draw a small horn on the top of its beak.
3. Draw one missing toe on each foot.
4. Draw the missing eyes.

Answer these questions by examining the completed triceratops.
1. Do you think this dinosaur was a meat-eating creature or a plant-eating creature? Why?

2. How do you think this dinosaur protected itself?

MY PET DINOSAUR

SYNTHESIS

Imagine that you have a pet dinosaur.
Write a story about what you would do to keep your pet dinosaur a secret.
Tell where you got the dinosaur, what you feed it, what you've named it,
and where you keep it.

WHAT HAPPENED?

EVALUATION

Dinosaurs are now extinct.

Scientists believe that dinosaurs might have become extinct because the earth became too cold, because a meteor crashed into the earth causing terrible fires, or because extreme weather conditions destroyed the food supply.

In the space below, draw a picture of what you think caused the dinosaurs to become extinct.

LEARNING BONUS

VOCABULARY

brachiosaurus
dinosaur
extinct
iguanodon
paleontologist

prehistoric
protection
protoceratops
skeleton

stegosaurus
trachodon
triceratops
tyrannosaurus

Dinosaur Search/Bulletin Board

Make a chart of dinosaur names for students to use in making original word find puzzles. Ask each student to make a dinosaur word find puzzle and answer key. Arrange the puzzles on a bulletin board with the answer keys in a folder in a corner of the board for self-checking. Students who are especially interested in dinosaurs may enjoy working in small groups to make matching or completion dinosaur puzzles.

Story Starters

Provide the students with the following list of story starters or have them create their own. Ask each student to choose one story starter and write a creative story to share with the class.

The teacher had just reached the exciting part of the story about the dinosaur searching for a home when . . .

Mrs. Wilkins could hardly believe her eyes when she climbed in the helicopter and found a baby dinosaur sitting in the front seat!

The truck carrying the largest dinosaur skeleton in the world came to a sudden halt when . . .

Puppet Parade

Provide the students with old socks, buttons, yarn, rickrack, and other "goodies" from the scrap box. Have the students use these materials to make creative dinosaur puppets. Allow time for small groups to work together to create and present puppet plays featuring their dinosaur puppets.

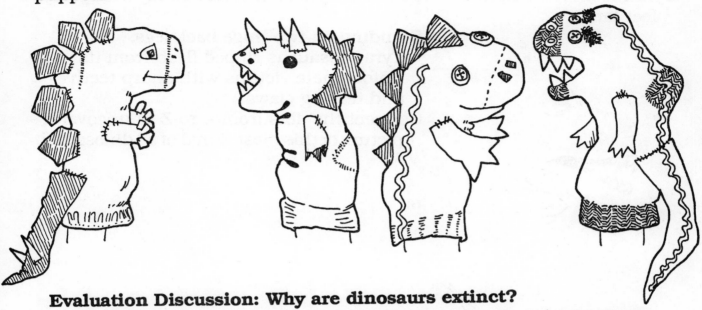

Evaluation Discussion: Why are dinosaurs extinct?

Lead a class discussion about why dinosaurs became extinct. Begin the session by reading several scientific selections. Then ask students to share their own theories and give reasons to support their ideas.

Dino-mite Homework Wrist Band

Have each student cut out this wrist band and write the following on it:

inside - One thing I've learned about dinosaurs is that scientists have not yet discovered why they became extinct.

outside - I'd like to tell you what I think happened to the dinosaurs. Then I'd like to hear what you think about it!

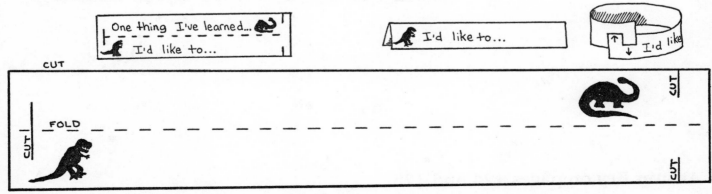

DINOSAUR DOT-TO-DOT

JUST FOR FUN

Tyrannosaurus is believed to have been the largest, most powerful flesh-eating creature to ever walk the earth.

Tyrannosaurus weighed more than seven tons and had a body nearly fifty feet long.

Standing on two huge back legs, Tyrannosaurus ripped flesh from its unfortunate victims with sharp teeth and tearing claws.

Connect the dots from A to Z to uncover a picture of this most feared of all dinosaurs!

Answer Key on pages 124 and 125.

INSECTS

UNIT AT A GLANCE

CONCEPT CAPSULE

Children will . . .
- become acquainted with the physical characteristics of several insects
- will be able to identify true insects
- understand that some insects are helpful to humans and some are harmful
- recognize and name insects in their environments
- gain an appreciation of insects as a part of the balance of nature

MATERIALS NEEDED

pencils, crayons, scissors, modeling clay, pipe cleaners, toothpicks, paint, paintbrushes, paste

ACTIVITIES

Knowledge: Legs, Legs, Legs
circle and color work sheet

Comprehension: Birth Of A Butterfly
drawing activity

Application: Insect Paste-ups
cut and paste work sheet

Analysis: Helpful Or Harmful?
identification work sheet

Synthesis: Backyard Collector
drawing activity

Evaluation: Compare The Insects
assessment activity

LEARNING BONUS

Vocabulary
Bugs Away/Bulletin Board
Insect Observation
Construct An Insect

Evaluation Discussion:
Choose An Insect
Happy Homework Wrist Band

JUST FOR FUN

Insects In The Air

LEGS, LEGS, LEGS

KNOWLEDGE

Every insect has six legs.
Circle each picture below of a critter that is not an insect.
Color the insects.

Answer Key on pages 124 and 125.

BIRTH OF A BUTTERFLY

COMPREHENSION

Most insects pass through four stages of growth: egg, larva,
    pupa, adult.

This growing process is called metamorphosis.

Draw the butterfly's metamorphosis below (use a reference
    book for help).

EGG

LARVA

PUPA

ADULT

INSECT PASTE-UPS
APPLICATION

All insects have three body parts, six legs and two antennae.
Cut out the body parts and legs below and paste them
together in the box to make a true insect.
Can you name this insect?

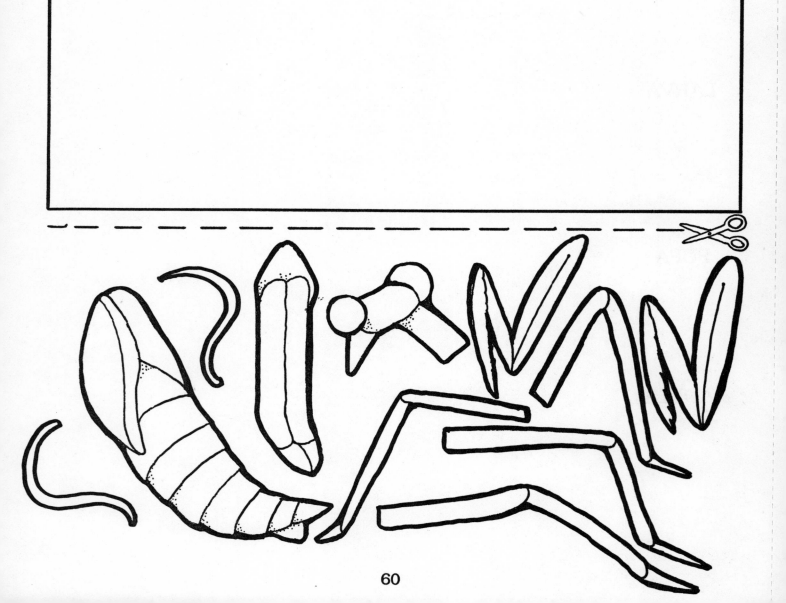

HELPFUL OR HARMFUL?

ANALYSIS

Some insects are helpful to humans and some are harmful.
Make an X on the pictures of harmful insects.
Tell how each of the other insects is helpful to humans.

bumblebee

clothes moth

termite

ladybug

butterfly

aphid

flea

dragonfly

BACKYARD COLLECTOR

SYNTHESIS

Pretend that you are an insect collector.
Draw a picture of the equipment you would need to catch an
  unusual insect in your backyard or on your school grounds.
Give this unusual insect a name and include the insect in
  the picture.

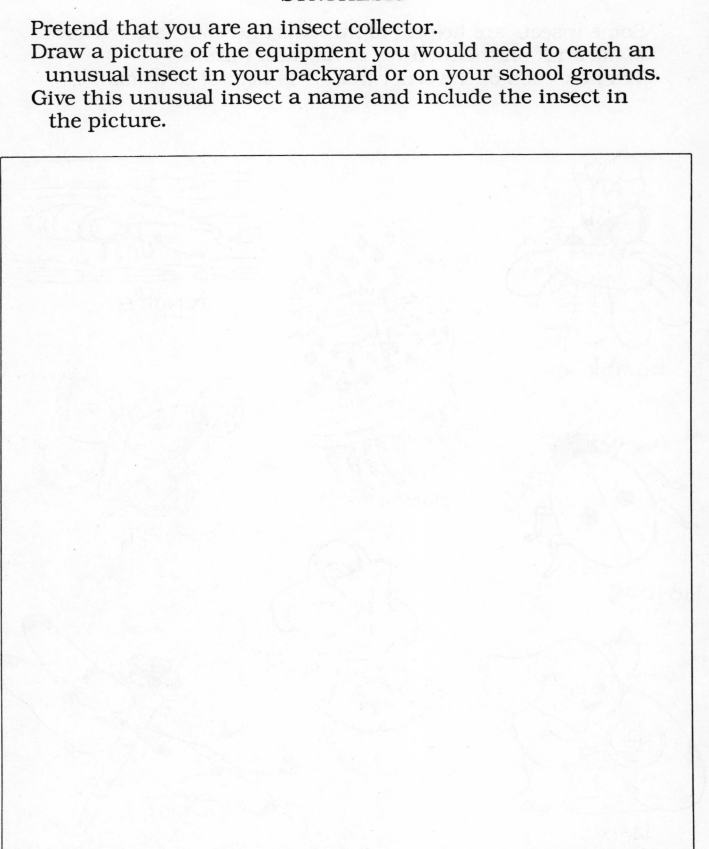

COMPARE THE INSECTS
EVALUATION

Color the picture and answer the questions.

1. Compare the three insects in the picture.
   How are they alike and how are they different?

2. Which of these insects would you most like to be?
   Give reasons for your choice.

3. Which of these insects is of greatest value to man?
   Give reasons for your choice.

LEARNING BONUS

WHY MOSQUITOES BUZZ IN PEOPLE'S EARS...

and what to do about it!

BUGG OFF!

BUGG OFF!

Bugs Away/Bulletin Board

Ask students to create a brand new bug spray to be used in the home, in the backyard or at the beach. Have each student write a newspaper or magazine ad to sell the product. Instruct students to invent a name for the spray and to design the packaging. Provide students with supplies for making posters to present their new products to the public. Cut out letters for the caption and display the posters on the board.

Insect Observation

Help students make insect inns. Have each student catch and observe an insect to learn three special things about the insect. Remind students that insect inns are for temporary stays only and that the insects are to be set free after the observation is complete.

rubber band

nylon hose

Construct An Insect

Provide students with pipe cleaners, toothpicks and modeling clay. Review the names and characteristics of several insects, reemphasizing that insects have three body parts, six legs, and two antennae. Ask each student to make an insect using the provided materials.

Evaluation Discussion: Choose An Insect

Discuss with students different types of insects and characteristics of each. Ask each student to name the insect he or she would most like to be and to give reasons for the choice.

Happy Homework Wrist Band

Have each student cut out this wrist band and write the following on it:

inside - All true insects have three body parts and six legs. Let's name six insects that are helpful to humans.

outside - Ask me to tell you how many body parts and how many legs an insect has.

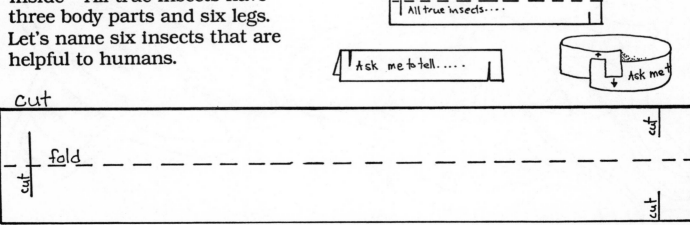

INSECTS IN THE AIR

JUST FOR FUN

Color and cut out the insects below.
Cut pieces of string to different lengths.
Attach one end of each piece of string to an insect and the other to a
   coat hanger to make an insect mobile.
Hang your mobile and enjoy watching your insects move!

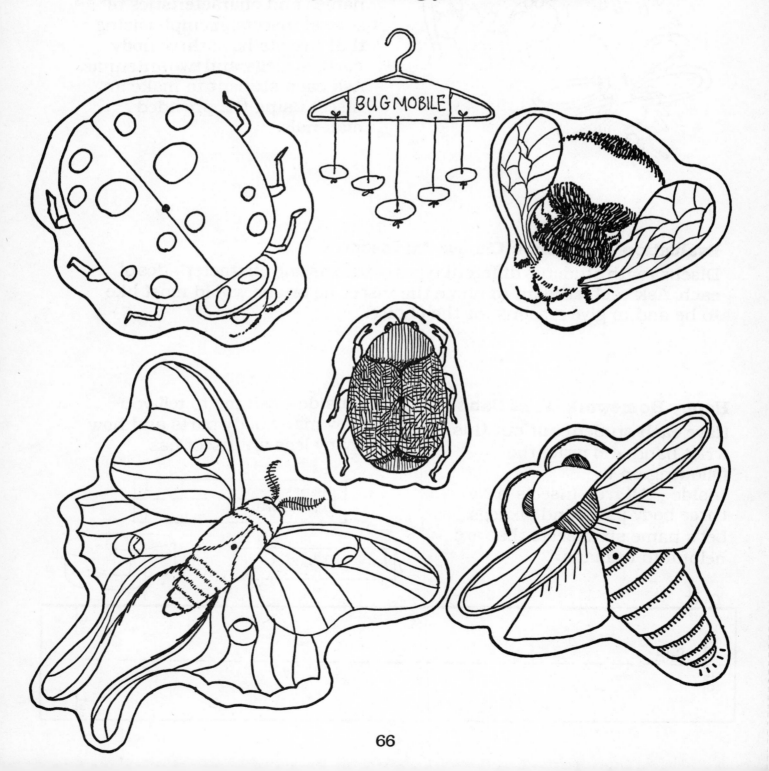

PLANTS

UNIT AT A GLANCE

CONCEPT CAPSULE
Children will . . .
- recognize and identify the six major plant parts
- understand that certain foods are actually parts of plants and will be able to name foods for each plant part
- gain an appreciation of the special ingredients and care needed for a healthy plant and garden
- understand that plants grow from seeds and pass through several stages before reaching maturation
- become familiar with the foods grown at different times of the year and the most suitable growing conditions for each food

MATERIALS NEEDED
scissors, paste, pencils, crayons, drawing paper, construction paper, seed catalogs and magazines, lima bean seeds, small pots, gallon pickle jar

ACTIVITIES
Knowledge: Plant Parts
cut and paste work sheet

Comprehension: Plants To Eat
matching/drawing activity

Application: Grow Your Own Plant
experimentation/observation work sheet

Analysis: Plants In Trouble
suggesting solutions

Synthesis: Seed Sensation
presenting an original idea

Evaluation: To Market, To Market
picture & questions work sheet

LEARNING BONUS
Vocabulary
A Seedy Show/Bulletin Board
You Can Learn A Lot From A Lima Bean
A Garden In A Jar
From Bud To Bloom

Evaluation Discussion:
    Favorite Fruits and Vegetables
Happy Homework Kitchen Caper

JUST FOR FUN
Plant Talk

PLANT PARTS

KNOWLEDGE

Plants can have six major parts: seed, root, stem, leaf, flower, and fruit.
Cut out the pictures below and paste them on another sheet of paper in
the correct order to show the development of a bell pepper from seed to
fruit.

 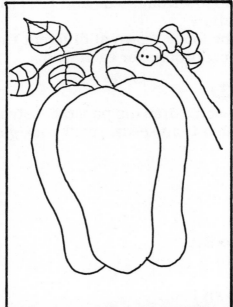 

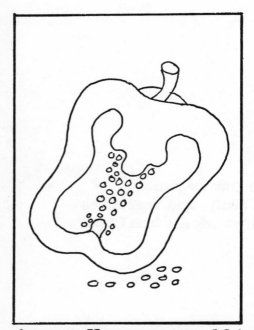  

Answer Key on pages 124 and 125.

PLANTS TO EAT

COMPREHENSION

Many parts of a plant may be eaten.
Draw lines to match each food with the plant part it represents.

flower   carrot
seed   lettuce
fruit   corn
stem   cauliflower
leaf   apple
root   celery

Draw a picture in the box below to show three of the foods listed above
  growing in a garden.

Color the picture.

Answer Key on pages 124 and 125.

GROW YOUR OWN PLANT

APPLICATION

Plant a few bean seeds in a milk carton or other container.
Water the seeds to help them grow.
Draw pictures below to show what your plant looks like at day 1, day 3, and day 5.

Day 1

Day 3

Day 5

PLANTS IN TROUBLE

ANALYSIS

Study the picture below.
Notice that many of the plants are not doing well.
Write three things that you could do to help the plants grow better.
Color the picture.

SEED SENSATION

SYNTHESIS

Invent a new seed and seed package.
Draw your special seed in box 1.
Draw the mature seed in its plant or
    flower stage in box 2.
Draw the seed package in box 3.

1.

2.

3.

TO MARKET, TO MARKET

EVALUATION

Study the picture of the fruit and vegetable stand below.
Answer the following questions.
Then color the picture.

1. Look at the fruits and vegetables in the picture below. Of which do you
   eat the:
   fruit? _____
   stem? _____
   leaf? _____
   root? _____
   seed? _____

2. Which fruit would you prefer to eat for dessert?
   _____

3. Which of the vegetables do you think are healthier to eat than others
   and why? _____

4. How do each of the following affect your selections when shopping for
   fruits and vegetables: color, texture, flavor, cost, preparation, serving
   temperature, and time of harvest?

   _____

CELERY SPECIAL 89¢

APPLES 1.00 DOZ

LETTUCE 79¢

POTATOES 1.00 DOZ

CARROTS 49¢ DOZ

ORANGES 2.50 DOZ

PEARS 2.98 DOZ

PEAS 1.25 lb.

1.50 pt.

FRESH STRAWBERRIES

BEANS 9¢ lb.

LEARNING BONUS

A Seedy Show/Bulletin Board

Ask students to bring different kinds of seeds to class for "show and tell." Encourage students to look for unusual seeds or ones which are not commonly thought of as seeds. Provide the class with seed catalogs and magazines. Help students locate and cut out pictures of plants that grow from seeds. Have each student make a poster to display on the bulletin board by pasting a seed and its corresponding picture on construction paper.

You Can Learn A Lot From A Lima Bean

Experiment to find out how air, water, and light affect the growth of plants.

1. Plant several lima beans in four pots.
   When the beans have sprouted, remove all but the healthiest plant from each pot.
2. Place one plant in the light and water it regularly.
3. Place one plant in the light but do not water it.
4. Tie a plastic bag around one plant to keep the air out, place it in the light and water it regularly.
5. Place one plant in the light but construct a cardboard blind around it to keep out the light. Water the plant regularly.
6. Keep a chart of the growth of the plants.

A Garden In A Jar

Plant cuttings in a pickle jar. (Clean the jar thoroughly before planting.) Place pebbles at the bottom of the jar and then add a layer of soil. Put the lid back on the jar and watch your garden grow!

From Bud To Bloom

Place twigs from trees or bushes in containers of water. Put the containers in a sunny window and watch the buds "unfold."

Evaluation Discussion: Favorite Fruits And Vegetables

Ask students to name plants they like to eat and to identify the part of the plant that is eaten. Encourage each student to consider the following factors for his or her chosen fruit or vegetable: color, texture, preparation, flavor, growing climate and season, cost to consumers, etc. Conclude the discussion by graphing the results on a chart.

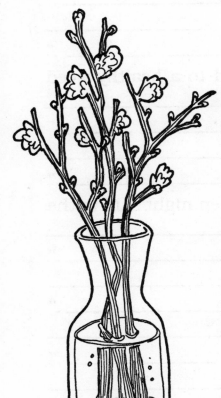

Happy Homework Kitchen Caper

Ask family members to help identify and list fruits and vegetables in the kitchen by the parts of the plant: flower, seed, fruit, stem, leaf and root.

PLANT TALK

JUST FOR FUN

Write a short dialogue for each of these make-believe talking plant situations.

1. A very old and very tall fir tree said to a tiny little evergreen, " _____
_____
_____."

The evergreen said, " _____
_____."

2. A beautiful rose bush dying from lack of care said to a healthy weed growing nearby, " _____
_____."

The weed said, " _____
_____."

3. The last pumpkin in the pumpkin patch on Halloween night said to the vine on which it was growing, " _____
_____."

The vine said, " _____
_____."

4. A potato said to an onion, " _____
_____."

The onion said, " _____
_____."

5. A shy little violet said to a proud lily, " _____
_____."

The lily said, " _____
_____."

FIVE SENSES

UNIT AT A GLANCE

CONCEPT CAPSULE
Children will . . .
- become familiar with the five senses and the functions of each
- become aware of the sensory impressions caused by everyday objects and the natural environment
- gain an appreciation of the importance of each of the five senses
- understand that the five senses allow us to be in contact with the physical world around us
- recognize the differences in pitch caused by the changes in physical elements

MATERIALS NEEDED
crayons and/or markers, sandpaper, sugar, water, oranges, aluminum foil, tree bark, pine needles, cotton candy, pencils, eight bottles for each student, various foods, paper bags

ACTIVITIES
Knowledge: It's Fun To Feel, See, Hear, Smell and Taste!
drawing activity

Comprehension: Experimenting With The Senses
observation experiment work sheet

Application: Sensory Scavenger Hunt
scavenger hunt work sheet

Analysis: Pop Bottle Pitch
pitch experiment work sheet

Synthesis: A Sense-able Feast
drawing activity

Evaluation: Scale Your Senses
ranking activity

LEARNING BONUS
Vocabulary
Sense-able Senses/Bulletin Board
A Collage With Feeling

IT'S FUN TO FEEL, SEE, HEAR, SMELL AND TASTE!

KNOWLEDGE

In each box below, draw pictures of three things you like to feel, see, hear, smell or taste.

FEEL	SEE
HEAR	**SMELL**
TASTE	

EXPERIMENTING WITH THE SENSES
COMPREHENSION

Use each of your five senses to examine these objects.
Your teacher will arrange the objects on a table for you.
Write words describing how each object looks, feels, smells, sounds or
   tastes (taste only the sugar, water, orange, and cotton candy) on the
   chart below.

Object	Looks (shape, color)	Feels	Smells	Sounds	Tastes
sandpaper	square, brown	rough	like dust	scratchy	X
sugar					
water					
orange					
aluminum foil					X
tree bark					X
pine needles					X
cotton candy					

SENSORY SCAVENGER HUNT

APPLICATION

Take a sensory scavenger hunt around your classroom, school and school grounds.

Look for an item which fits each description below.

Bring the items back to class in a paper bag or write notes about each item.

Discuss your chosen items with the class.

1. something nice to look at
2. something unpleasant to taste
3. something cold to touch
4. something pretty to hear
5. something impossible to smell

6. something rough to touch
7. something bright to see
8. something quiet to listen to
9. something good to smell
10. something smooth to touch

Notes about items:

POP BOTTLE PITCH

ANALYSIS

Ask your teacher for eight pop bottles (or other bottles) of the same size.
Fill each bottle with a different amount of water.
Record the amount of water in each bottle by coloring the bottles below to
  show the amounts.
Blow across each bottle and then answer the questions below.

1. How do the bottles sound?

   _____

2. Which bottle makes the highest sound?

   _____

3. Which bottle makes the lowest sound?

   _____

4. What happens to the sound each bottle makes after adding water to
   the bottle?

   _____

5. What vibrates to produce the sounds you hear?

   _____

6. Define the word "pitch."

   _____

Arrange the bottles in order from the highest pitch to the lowest pitch.

A SENSE-ABLE FEAST

SYNTHESIS

Pretend that you are to create a special feast which is appealing to each of
the five senses.
Choose foods that . . .

- are colorful
- have eye appeal
- vary in texture
- taste salty, sour, sweet and bitter
- make special sounds as they are cooked
- smell delicious as they are cooking or baking

Draw your appealing meal on the table below.

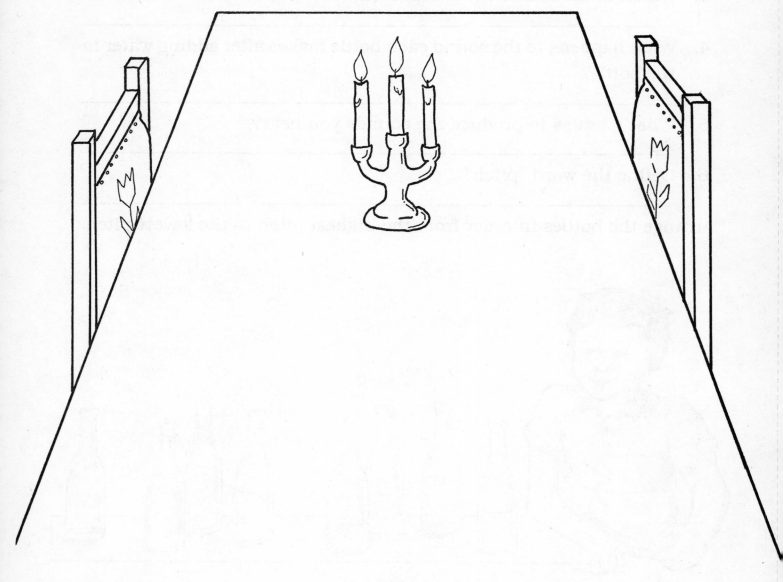

SCALE YOUR SENSES

EVALUATION

Look at each group of pictures below.
Follow the directions for each picture group.

1. Put a 1 beside the picture of the most unpleasant sound, a 3 beside the picture of the most pleasant sound, and a 2 beside the remaining picture.

2. Put a 1 beside the picture of the least desirable thing to look at, a 3 beside the picture of the most pleasing thing to look at, and a 2 beside the remaining picture.

3. Put a 1 beside the picture of the most unpleasant smell, a 3 beside the picture of the most appealing smell, and a 2 beside the remaining picture.

4. Put a 1 beside the picture of the most unpleasant object to touch, a 3 beside the most desirable object to touch, and a 2 beside the remaining picture.

5. Put a 1 beside the picture of the most unpleasant food to taste, a 3 beside the picture of the least unpleasant food to taste, and a 2 beside the remaining picture.

LEARNING BONUS

Sense-able Senses/Bulletin Board

Ask the class to help you create a bulletin board which illustrates how the five senses protect us from harm. Discuss ways that our senses protect us such as stoplights and stop signs preventing traffic accidents (sight), smoke alarms and smoke warning us of fire (hearing and smell), etc. Have students draw pictures of ways that the five senses can serve as means of protection and display them on the bulletin board. Group the pictures according to each of the five senses and label each group.

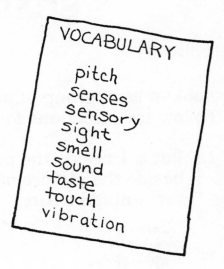

A Collage With Feeling

Have each student make a texture collage to explore the sense of touch! Ask students to bring items with different textures to class such as cotton, sandpaper, aluminum foil, carpet scraps, buttons, etc. Instruct the students to glue their items on large pieces of construction paper. Display the completed collages in a "sensory exploration center" where students may go to explore texture. A collection of instruments that make sounds such as bells, a xylophone, a whistle, cymbals, a toy drum, etc. may be added to extend the use of the center to the exploration of sound.

HEALTH AND NUTRITION

UNIT AT A GLANCE

CONCEPT CAPSULE

Children will . . .

- know the four food groups and be able to name foods in each group
- become familiar with the important nutritional benefits of eating foods from each food group
- understand that a well-balanced, nutritious meal which includes foods from each food group is necessary in order to achieve and maintain a healthy body
- realize that certain foods can be harmful to the body when eaten in excess
- practice making wise food choices

MATERIALS NEEDED

scissors, paste, pencils, crayons, magazines, construction paper

ACTIVITIES

Knowledge: Plan A Meal
cut and paste activity

Comprehension: Lunch Box Dilemma
drawing activity

Application: Appetizing Puppets
finger puppet activity

Analysis: Something's Missing
completion/drawing work sheet

Synthesis: Delicious Riddles
riddle solving activity

Evaluation: Meals For A Week
meal planning activity

LEARNING BONUS

Vocabulary
Menu Magic/Bulletin Board
Evaluation Discussion: Be A Smart Shopper
Recipe Roundup

PLAN A MEAL

KNOWLEDGE

Cut out pictures of several foods below and paste them on the table to make a delicious, well-balanced meal.

Be sure to include food from each of the four food groups.

LUNCH BOX DILEMMA

COMPREHENSION

Laura must make her own lunch for school today.
She has chosen too many of the same kinds of foods.
Make an X on the food items that Laura should not pack in her lunch.
Draw pictures of more nutritious foods that she could include.

APPETIZING PUPPETS

APPLICATION

Color and cut out the four finger puppets below.
Use the puppets to present a play about the four food groups.

SOMETHING'S MISSING

ANALYSIS

Examine each plate below.
Decide which food group is not there.
Draw a food from the missing food group on each plate.

DELICIOUS RIDDLES

SYNTHESIS

Guess what food each riddle below describes.

I am red or brown
And I'm grown in the ground;
I also have eyes
And I can be French fries.
What am I?

I come in all colors
And I have a tail;
I wear fins and scales
And swim with the whales.
What am I?

I am purple or green,
You find me in bunches;
I am round and juicy
And I'm found in school lunches.
What am I?

Now make up a food riddle of your own!

MEALS FOR A WEEK

EVALUATION

Recommend a balanced diet plan for your family.
Choose foods from each of the four food groups for three meals for five
   days.
Write the meals in the chart below.
Try to plan a variety of meals with as many different foods as you can.
Ask your family to use the diet plan for a week!

	MONDAY	TUESDAY	WEDNESDAY	THURSDAY	FRIDAY
Breakfast					
Lunch					
Dinner					

LEARNING BONUS

Menu Magic/Bulletin Board

Cut out pictures of foods in the four food groups from magazines. Display these pictures according to their respective food groups on the bulletin board and label each group. Ask the students to collect menus from their favorite restaurants. Arrange the menus on the board. Study the menus as a class to determine which one lists the healthiest foods. Suggest criteria for determining this if necessary.

Evaluation Discussion: Be A Smart Shopper

Have the class discuss wise food choices by answering these questions.

1. Name foods that make nutritious snacks.
2. Name foods that should always be kept cool.
3. Name foods that should be cooked before you eat them.
4. Name foods that would be good picnic items.
5. What do you and your family look for when choosing a supermarket or grocery store? Consider size, location, service, prices, and parking.

Recipe Roundup

Ask each student to bring a nutritious family recipe to share with the class. During sharing time, discuss the components of each recipe to determine the food value of each as well as the food groups represented. Duplicate the recipes to compile a cookbook for each student. Extend the learning fun by staging a contest for the best name and cover design for the cookbook.

EXPLORE A BICYCLE

Materials

bicycle
dictionary
encyclopedia
pencils
crayons
drawing paper
miscellaneous art
  supplies

EXPLORATION CHALLENGES

1. Find the definition of bicycle in the dictionary. Find at least three other words that begin with "bi." Write the words.

2. Draw pictures of a bicycle, a unicycle, and a tricycle. Consult a dictionary or encyclopedia if you need help.

3. Make a list of six words which describe a bicycle. Read your list to a friend and see if he or she can guess what you are describing.

4. List two ways a bicycle is like . . .

   a wheelbarrow
   a lawn mower
   a skateboard

5. Give three reasons why a boy or girl of your age should own a bicycle.

6. Turn one wheel of a bicycle and count the spokes. Why do you think the bicycle has that number of spokes?

7. Slowly turn one of the pedals of a bicycle. Use three sentences or less to describe the pedals so that someone who has never seen a bicycle pedal could draw a picture of it.

8. Make up a television commercial to sell a bicycle.

9. Write a letter to someone in your class describing a super bicycle that is the world's "most wanted" bicycle.

EXPLORATION CHALLENGES

10. Design a basket for a bicycle which would hold a picnic lunch, a change of clothes, an umbrella and your school books.

11. Which of these people do you think has the most need for a bicycle?
    a. a newspaper delivery boy
    b. a third grade student
    c. a teacher who lives three miles from school and has no car

12. Give three ways a bicycle is different from a motorcycle.

13. Plan a bicycle race for your class. How far will you race? When, where and how will the race take place? What will be the prize?

14. How are bicycle brakes important? Write a sentence to tell what could happen if bicycles had no brakes.

15. Make a list of safety rules that you think would prevent most bicycle injuries.

16. Do you think bicycle owners should have to buy operator's licenses? Give two reasons why they should or should not.

17. Draw a picture of a bicycle designed for a black bear.

18. Draw a picture of a bicycle that might belong to a boy or girl living on another planet.

EXPLORE COLOR

Materials

markers
drawing paper of various sizes
magazines and catalogs
glue
scissors
pencils
poster board

big box of crayons
  (as many colors as possible)
dictionary
encyclopedia
watercolors
paints

EXPLORATION CHALLENGES

1. Use an encyclopedia to find out how science helps us understand color. Draw or paint a picture to illustrate your findings. Write a sentence or two for each picture to answer these questions:

   - Why are plants green?
   - What makes a rainbow?
   - What causes color blindness?

2. Look up the words hue, chroma, and value in the dictionary and find out how each relates to color. Make a color chart by painting or coloring a swatch or patch at the top of a piece of drawing paper for each color. Browse through magazines and catalogs to find many different hues of each color. Cut out the pictures and glue them on the appropriate color papers.

3. Make a list of the primary and secondary colors. Write other words that are shades or hues of each color.

   Example: Green

   a. mint
   b. turquoise
   c. emerald

4. Complete five of the color comparisons below. Refer to a dictionary if you need help.

   - Chartreuse is like . . . .
   - Scarlet is like . . . .
   - Aqua is like . . . .
   - Lavender is like . . . .
   - Beige is like . . . .
   - Turquoise is like . . . .
   - Magenta is like . . . .
   - Sienna is like . . . .

5. See how many different colors you can create by mixing the colors blue, red, yellow and black. Use crayons or paints.

6. Draw a large circle on white poster board. Color the circle with many bright colors. Insert a pencil through the center of the circle and spin it like a top on a smooth surface. What do you see?

7. Perform a science experiment to answer one of these questions.

   - What color best reflects or absorbs sunlight?
   - What colors attract birds, insects and house pets?
   - What colors make white?
   - Can a prism teach you about color? How?

8. Paint or color a large butterfly or other insect so that it will blend in with its natural surroundings. Hide the insect outside in the bushes, grass, flowers, etc. See how long it takes a friend to find it.

9. Divide the colors in the investigation center into "cool colors" and "warm colors." Design a piece of wrapping paper using only warm or cool colors.

97

EXPLORATION CHALLENGES

12. Make a coat of arms for your family using this color meanings chart for reference.

    yellow or gold - cheerfulness
    brown - hard-working
    black - sadness
    white - religious
    red - love
    orange - honesty
    purple - royalty
    green - creative

11. What three colors are most like you? What colors best "illustrate" your personality? Use "your colors" to make a button, bumper sticker or crest which tells something important about you.

10. Go outside and find examples of things in nature for as many colors as you can. Make a color list of these things.

15. Use each of these colorful expressions in a sentence. Color or paint a picture to show what each means. Be creative!

    ● Seeing red
    ● White as a sheet
    ● Tickled pink
    ● Green thumb

14. Plan a color party for your family or friends. Use crayons or watercolors to design a menu, invitations, decorations, place cards and games.

13. Plan a coloring contest for your family or friends. Consider what coloring tools to use -- magic markers, crayons, watercolors, paints, or colored pencils. Decide who can enter, what the rules should be, and what the prize will be. Think about who should judge the contest and what the criteria for judging should include.

18. Imagine what the world would be like if everything were yellow. Write your feelings in a brief paragraph.

17. Draw and color several flags using primary colors only. Design a flag for your state, your school, your country, your house, your pet, and yourself!

16. For each word below, choose a color which you feel represents it best.

    anger   freedom
    fear   safety
    happiness   summer
    rain   illness

98

EXPLORE MAGNETS

Materials

encyclopedia
dictionary
book about magnets
index cards
pencils
eraser
paper clips
penny

nail
hairpin
comb (plastic)
can tab
pebble
string
scissors
box

piece of plastic
aluminum foil
glass
cardboard
jar with lid
steel wool

EXPLORATION CHALLENGES

1. Use an encyclopedia, dictionary, or library book about magnets to find out what each of these words means.

   poles
   attract
   repel
   compass
   magnetic field
   magnetic force

2. Make a set of flashcards about magnets. Write five true facts on five cards and five false facts on five cards. Shuffle the cards and ask a friend to determine which facts are true and which are false.

3. Predict whether or not a magnet will attract each of these items: pencil, eraser, paper clip, penny, paper, nail, hairpin, comb, can tab, and pebble. Touch a magnet to each to see if your predictions were right. Give yourself three points for each correct prediction. If your score is 24 or more, you are a magnet whiz! If your score is less than 24, research to find out more about magnets.

4. Conduct a magnet survey in your home. Walk through each room in your house and look for as many uses of magnets as you can. Record your findings. Then, see how many objects you can pick up with one magnet in only five minutes!

5. Create a science experiment or magic trick using magnets. Demonstrate your experiment or trick for family, friends and classmates.

6. Make a list of machines which use magnets in some way to clean, cook, repair, build, and entertain. (Remember, anything with an electric motor uses magnets!)

7. Estimate the number of paper clips each of two magnets will pick up. Then conduct an experiment to see how accurate your estimates were.

8. Make a "fishing" game. Draw ten fish on paper and cut them out. Slip a paper clip through the mouth of each fish. On each fish write one question about magnets and a number. Write the answers to each numbered question on a separate paper. Put the fish in a box. Make a fishing pole using a pencil, string and a magnet. Try to catch a fish and answer the question!

9. For this experiment you will need paper, plastic, aluminum foil, glass, cardboard, and a sheet of steel (such as a shelving unit, etc.). Place a paper clip on top of an item and hold a magnet beneath the item. Move the magnet back and forth. Does the paper clip follow the magnet? Follow this procedure for every item to see if the magnetic attraction passes through the item.

EXPLORATION CHALLENGES

10. Sprinkle iron filings onto a piece of cardboard. Hold one or more magnets under the cardboard and move the iron filings around to make an original picture. Can you explain what scientific principle makes the iron filings form a picture?

11. Pretend that you are a magnet walking through a junkyard. Write a paragraph about all of the things that happen to you during the walk. Use such words as poles, attract, repel, force field, and magnetize.

12. Design a new and unusually shaped magnet for your refrigerator.

13. If you were to teach someone about magnets, what would be the three most important things you would want the person to know?

14. List all of the reasons you can think of why magnets are important.

15. Experiment with several magnets and record your findings in report form. See what happens when you place two magnets end to end. Try to stack several magnets and note the results. Experiment with the magnets by trying to attract many different kinds of objects. Try to determine the maximum weight that one magnet will hold.

16. Make your own "magnet metal detector" game. Fill a shallow box with sand and hide several metal objects and non-metal objets in the sand. Move the magnet over the surface and try to uncover the hidden treasures!

17. Write a poem about magnets which compares magnets to other things, ideas or people. Illustrate the poem.

18. Make a collage of pictures cut from magazines that show objects or machines which use magnets.

EXPLORE A MICROSCOPE

Materials

microscope
paper (white, black)
pencils
dictionary
encyclopedia
file cards
soda crackers
piece of cloth

salt
ink pad
spices
aluminum foil
straight pins
water in a jar
crayons or markers

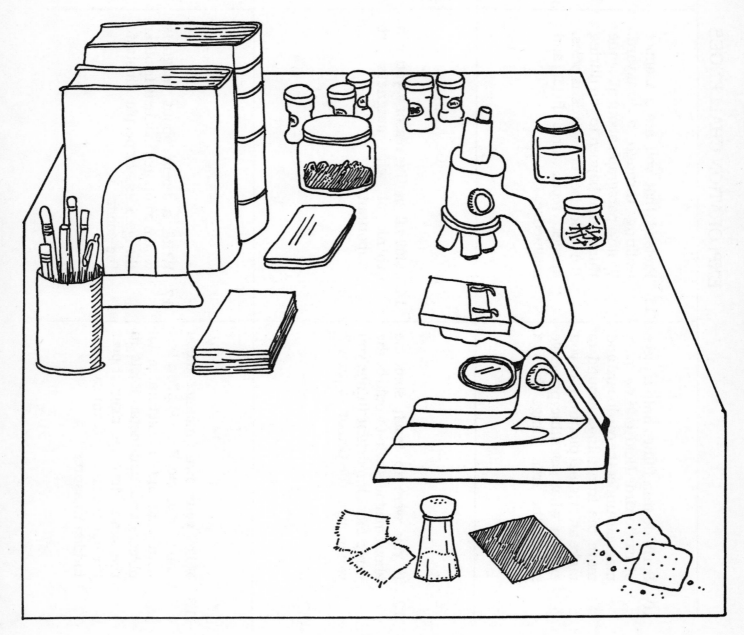

EXPLORATION CHALLENGES

1. Use a dictionary or encyclopedia to find out why a microscope is called a "microscope." Find at least three other words in the dictionary that begin with "micro." Write the words.

2. Make a list of six words which describe a microscope. Read your list to a friend and see if he or she can guess what you are describing.

3. If you had to draw a microscope so that someone else would recognize it, would you draw it from the front or the side? Draw a microscope.

4. List all the ways a microscope is like . . .
   - a pair of glasses
   - a pair of eyes
   - a pair of mirrors

5. Write three reasons why it is good to have a microscope in the classroom.

6. Keep a record of your microscopic observations on file cards. Record these things on each card:
   - examination number
   - date of examination
   - object examined
   - where I found the object
   - my observations
   - other remarks

7. Look at the surfaces of small pieces of cracker under a microscope. How are the pieces alike and different? Draw what you see.

8. Look at a piece of cloth under a microscope. Draw a picture of how the threads look.

9. Sprinkle salt on a piece of black paper and look at it under the microscope. What do you see? Put a few drops of water on the salt and increase the magnification. What happens to the salt?

103

EXPLORATION CHALLENGES

12. Press your thumb on an ink pad and then on a piece of paper to make a thumb print. Look at the print under the microscope. What kind of print do you have?

15. You will need one 3" x 3" square piece of aluminum foil for this experiment. Use a pin to make a small hole in the foil. Drop a small amount of water in the hole. Place an object under the foil and examine it. Is it magnified? How does the water compare to the lens of a microscope?

18. Write a description of a microscope for someone who has never seen one before.

11. Bring a spoonful of soil from your yard to class on a small piece of white paper and look at it under the microscope. Describe what you see.

14. Make your own facsimile microscope. Make a pinhole in the corner of a file card. Put the pinhole close to your eye and look closely at some printed material. What happens?

17. If you were a microscope, what would you say to . . .

- a bug?
- a mirror?
- a scientist?
- a pebble?

10. Select ten small items to examine under the microscope such as a coin, an eraser, a picture, etc. Group the items according to different criteria such as color, size and shape.

13. Look at several spices under the microscope. What shapes do they have? What colors do they have? How do the spices differ?

16. Complete these ideas about microscopes.

- A microscope is important because . . .
- A microscope can be used for . . .
- A microscope is made of . . .
- A microscope must never be . . .
- A microscope can show us . . .

EXPLORE AN OCTASCOPE

Materials

octascope
drawing paper
pencils
metric measuring stick
dictionary

EXPLORATION CHALLENGES

3. What five words best describe an octascope? Write them in alphabetical order.

6. Using a dictionary, find the definitions of scope, octagon, cylinder, "tele," concave, and convex.

9. Look through the octascope and focus on one object. Rotate the octascope. What changes occur?

2. Look through an octascope. Draw a geometric design that you saw.

5. How many lines intersect in the middle of the octascope?

8. Count the number of revolutions it takes for your octascope to roll from one end of the table to the other.

1. What is the shape of an octascope? Draw an octascope as technically correct as you can. Look at an actual octascope or a picture for reference.

4. What observations can you make when looking through the end opposite the eyepiece of an octascope?

7. Make a list of the materials you would need to construct your own octascope.

EXPLORATION CHALLENGES

10. How is an octascope like a telescope? How is it different?

11. How is an octascope like a work of art?

12. Describe the difference between an octascope and a kaleidoscope.

13. Use a metric measure to record the length, circumference, and diameter of an octascope.

14. Using the octascope as a measure, measure the length of the chalkboard, the teacher's desk, and the top of a bookcase.

15. Look into the octascope. Then ask a friend to look through the octascope. Each of you write a brief paragraph describing what you saw. Compare your paragraphs.

16. Write a short story about a magical octascope.

17. Find at least five words in the dictionary that begin with "octa." Write the definitions of these words.

18. Write a paragraph describing an octascope in as much detail as you can. Compare your paragraph with the paragraphs of several classmates. Is your description like or different from the others? How do the perspectives differ?

EXPLORE A PERISCOPE

Materials

periscope
several mirrors
drawing paper
pencils
tape

scissors
small pictures
cardboard tubes
one quart paper milk cartons
dictionary

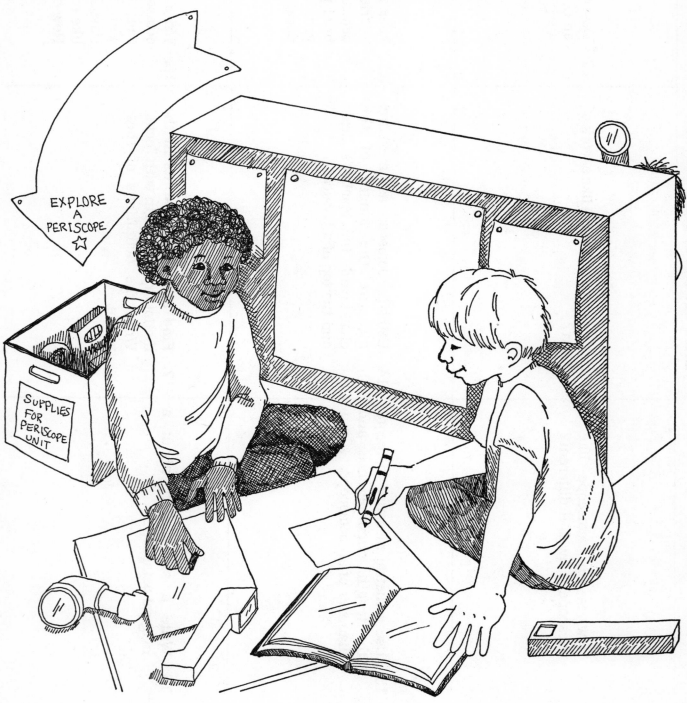

EXPLORATION CHALLENGES

1. An important part of a periscope is the set of two mirrors. Find the mirrors in a periscope. What do you see when you look into a mirror? Draw a picture of what you see.

2. Put two mirrors together end to end, keeping them flat. What do you see? Turn the mirrors toward each other a little more ($\smile$) and draw what you see. Turn the mirrors toward each other a little more ($\vee$) and draw what you see. Turn the mirrors toward each other even more ($\vee$) and draw what you see. How many objects can you see?

3. Place a mirror on top of a small picture. How does the picture look? Turn the picture upside down. How does the picture look in the mirror? Turn the picture sideways. How does it look in the mirror now?

4. Hold two mirrors about three inches apart. Place an object between the mirrors. How does the object look?

5. Draw a design on a small piece of paper (about the size of a 3" x 5" card). Cut the design in half. Place the cut side of the design next to a mirror which is standing upright. Draw what you see in the mirror.

6. Fit one mirror into a cardboard tube. Look through the tube. What do you see? Look into the mirror end and move the tube from side to side. What do you see now? Turn the tube around so that the mirror is up, down, left and right. Draw what you see.

7. Make your own periscope! You will need a one-quart paper milk container, two small mirrors, tape and scissors.
   a. Cut a hole at each end of the tube or container. Make sure that the holes are on opposite sides and opposite ends.
   b. Tape a mirror opposite each hole inside the tube. Make sure each mirror is at a 40° angle to the hole.

8. Stand with a large mirror behind you. Look through the periscope. What do you see?

9. Get under a table with a periscope. Can you see an object that is on the table? What does the object look like?

10. Have a friend stand around a corner. Use your periscope to try to see your friend.

11. Ask a friend to draw a star on the chalkboard. Can you find the star while looking through the periscope? Draw a picture that shows the position of your periscope when you found the star.

12. Look through your periscope to find yourself. What do you see? Can you move the periscope so that you can see your face?

13. Make as many different words as you can using the letters in the word periscope. Write the words and check their spellings in a dictionary.

14. Use a dictionary to find as many words as you can that end in "scope." How many words did you find? Try to figure out what "scope" means by examining the words you found in the dictionary.

15. Who uses a periscope? Where would a periscope be helpful? Use an encyclopedia for help if you wish.

16. Ask your teacher for permission to take the periscope outside to experiment with it. Record the events and findings of your "research" in report form.

17. Write an adventure story which involves a periscope. Illustrate the story and share it with the class.

18. How is a periscope like a microscope, a telescope, and an octascope? Write your findings in paragraph form.

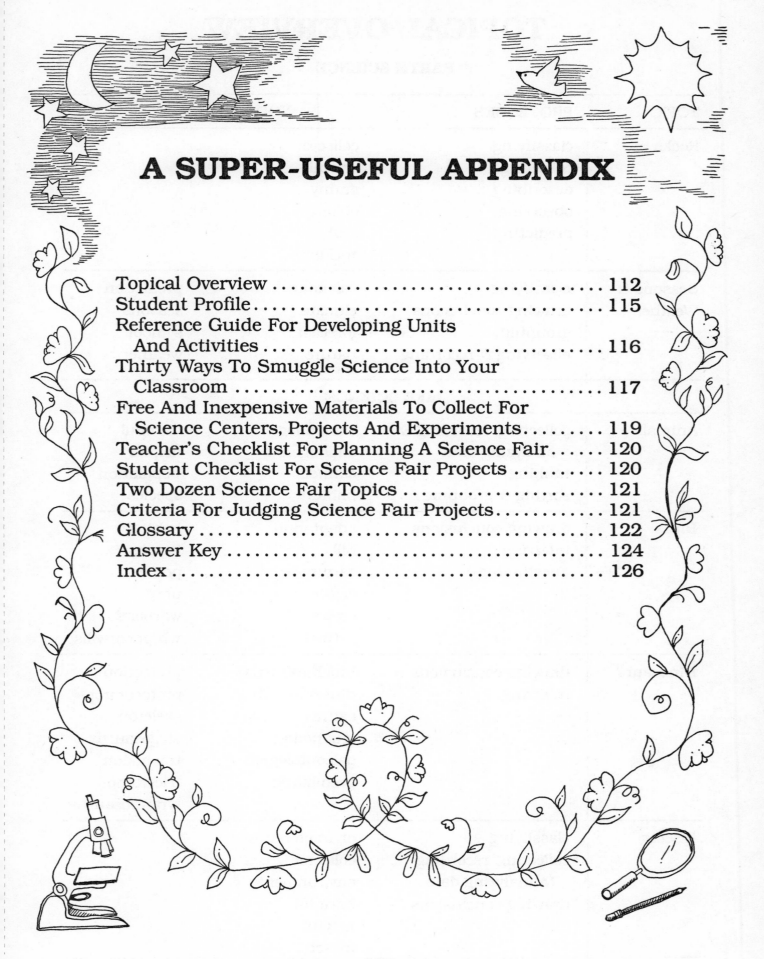

A SUPER-USEFUL APPENDIX

TOPICAL OVERVIEW

EARTH SCIENCE

TOPIC	PROCESSES	VOCABULARY	
Rocks	classifying collecting describing observing predicting	collector crystal grainy oblong oval rocks	
Seasons & Weather	classifying drawing conclusions grouping observing & recording	calendar climate forecast nature	prediction seasons symbol weather

LIFE SCIENCE

TOPIC	PROCESSES	VOCABULARY	
Animals	collecting, recording & analyzing data ranking sorting & grouping	camouflage endangered extinct habitat	harmful helpful population species
Birds	drawing conclusions inferring questioning	adaptation bill cardinals crown crows extinct	habitat herons perch prey warblers whippoorwills
Dinosaurs	drawing conclusions inferring	brachiosaurus dinosaur extinct iguanodon paleontologist prehistoric	protection protoceratops skeleton stegosaurus trachodon triceratops tyrannosaurus
Insects	classifying collecting, recording & analyzing data drawing conclusions	characteristics collector environment harmful helpful insect	

112

TOPIC	PROCESSES	VOCABULARY		
Plants	classifying drawing conclusions experimenting identifying problems & solutions observing	flower fruit garden leaf root seed	stem texture vegetable	
Five Senses	classifying describing examining experimenting rank ordering	pitch senses sensory sight smell	sound taste touch vibration	
Health & Nutrition	drawing conclusions identifying problems & solutions	balanced diet calcium four food groups iron	minerals nutrition vitamins	

PHYSICAL SCIENCE

TOPIC	PROCESSES	VOCABULARY		
Bicycles	collecting, recording, & analyzing data describing observing predicting questioning	bicycle brakes license motorcycle pedals	spokes tricycle unicycle wheelbarrow	
Color	collecting, recording & analyzing data drawing conclusions experimenting observing questioning	chroma color color blindness hue litmus paper primary colors secondary colors swatch value		

TOPIC	PROCESSES	VOCABULARY	
Magnets	collecting, recording, & analyzing data describing drawing conclusions experimenting observing predicting questioning	attract compass magnetic field magnetic force magnetism magnets poles repel	

ALL SCIENCES

TOPIC	PROCESSES	VOCABULARY	
Microscopes	collecting, recording & analyzing data comparing drawing conclusions experimenting observing predicting questioning	facsimile lens magnification microscope	
Octascopes	collecting, recording & analyzing data comparing experimenting measuring	circumference concave convex cylinder diameter focus geometric	kaleidoscope octagon octascope scope
Periscopes	collecting, recording & analyzing data comparing experimenting observing	angle periscope scope	

STUDENT PROFILE

Student	Activity	Date Started	Date Completed	Rating

Rating code: (1) non-satisfactory, (2) satisfactory, (3) good,

(4) very good, (5) superior

REFERENCE GUIDE FOR
DEVELOPING UNITS AND ACTIVITIES

STAGES	TRIGGER VERBS	
KNOWLEDGE recalling, restating, and remembering learned information	choose find group identify know label list match memorize	read recall recite select what when where who write
COMPREHENSION grasping meaning of information by interpreting and translating learnings	change compose contrast define draw	estimate explain group retell show
APPLICATION making use of information in a context different from the one in which it was learned	choose classify construct experiment interview	produce prove record select
ANALYSIS breaking learned information into its component parts	classify compare contrast discover	divide examine inspect take apart
SYNTHESIS creating new information and ideas using previous learnings	build combine compose construct create design	develop imagine invent make up rearrange
EVALUATE making judgments about learned information on basis of established criteria	decide grade judge measure	rank rate select test

THIRTY WAYS TO SMUGGLE SCIENCE INTO YOUR CLASSROOM

Use these simple process skills activities to "stretch the minds and tease the imaginations" of young scientists.

1. Pretend you are a cloud on a windy day. Describe your adventures.
2. Imagine what it would be like to be an insect. Which insect would you prefer to be and why?
3. Give three reasons why science can be fun.
4. Develop a plan to help people quit smoking.
5. Be a snake in the grass and draw an ideal habitat from your point of view.
6. Invent a machine to do a simple chore for you at home. Draw a picture of the machine and describe how it works.
7. What machine do you wish had never been invented? Give a good reason for your choice.
8. Design an energy conservation bumper sticker.
9. Imagine how Thomas Edison would react to a video arcade.
10. List all of the ways you can think of to use a rock for a tool.
11. List as many things as you can that measure other things.
12. Find a picture of a seasonal change and add details to it.
13. Write three good questions to ask in order to find out more about weather.
14. Write two questions that would have the answer "pollution."
15. Draw a picture to show what you think you would find in outer space as the first student traveling to Mars.

16. Which do you find more fascinating, the sky or the sea? Why?
17. Write as many uses for a pulley as you can.
18. Think about a scientific phenomenon that baffles you such as rust, a rainbow, fog or tides. Try to figure out an explanation for it.
19. If your science textbook could talk, what would it say?
20. Which is more interesting to you, a high mountain or a high tide? Why?
21. Pretend that you are a weed that people are trying to destroy. Tell a story about your life.
22. What do you think would happen if you put Alka-Seltzer in a corked soda bottle full of warm water? Try it and see!
23. Invent an original story about a caterpillar.
24. If you had hands for feet, how would your life be changed?
25. Pretend that you are a bird and speculate what you would like to know about people.
26. Which do you think came first, the chicken or the egg?
    Explain your answer.
27. Imagine what life would be like without the invention of the wheel. Write your ideas.
28. Describe ways that you would like to improve your school science program.
29. Pretend that you just ate a hamburger. Draw the route that it will take through your digestive tract.
30. Tell about two different ways that people have altered the environment. Classify these changes as good or bad and justify your choices.

FREE AND INEXPENSIVE MATERIALS TO COLLECT FOR SCIENCE CENTERS, PROJECTS AND EXPERIMENTS

- **aluminum pie tins** - for sorting, storing, categorizing and displaying collections (seeds, rocks, shells, etc.); for mixing colors, liquids, solids; for water and soil experiments

- **empty bottles** - for rooting plant cuttings, experimenting with sound (pitch), and conducting water pollution experiments

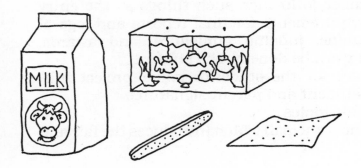

- **waxed and paper milk cartons** - for measuring, holding collections, and potting plants

- **boxes of assorted shapes and sizes** - for holding collections; making peep boxes, dioramas, and individual science tool kits; and for general storage

- **nylon hose** - for tops of insect cages and for binding plant stems (cut hosiery into strips)

- **6-pak holder** - for holding science tools and collections (especially good for this because it's portable)

- **glass jars** - for making terrariums, aquariums, and vivariums; for measuring; for holding water during experiments; and for see-through storage for collections and supplies

- **sponges** - for quick cleanup, growing and observing grass seed, and water experimentation (absorption, floatation)

- **corks** - for use in floatation experiments and use as stoppers for bottled liquids

- **nails, screws, washers** - for experiments, displays, and discussions of other uses

- **sandpaper, emery board, drinking straws, ice cream spoons, plastic picnic utensils, tongue depressors** - for experiments, projects, and displays

- **metric and standard measuring tapes; scales; old alarm clock** - for general use in measuring lengths, widths, heights, and time

- **plastic butter and cottage cheese containers with plastic tops** - for potting plants and temporarily storing insects or small animals (be sure to punch air holes in the tops when used to house living things)

- **string, rubber bands, fishing cord, yarn, elastic** - for experiments and miscellaneous projects

- **scrap lumber, wood shavings, and dowel sticks** - for experiments and miscellaneous uses

- **large cardboard boxes, corrugated cardboard, shirt boards and tagboard** - for making exhibits, signs, and posters

- **paper bags, small shopping bags and plastic sandwich and utility bags** - for storage, experiments, and displays

TEACHER'S CHECKLIST FOR PLANNING A SCIENCE FAIR

1. Determine the main objectives of the science fair.
2. Recruit volunteers (teachers and parents) who have good organizational skills and an interest in science to serve on the science fair committee.
3. Set a time, location, and date for the science fair (schedule it to be about four to five months after the first committee meeting). Clear the date with the principal.
4. Write the science fair rules. Remember to include such things as the entry deadline, size limits for displays, requirements for final reports and logs of observations, the completion deadline, judging guidelines, and awards. Emphasize the requirement that all work be done by the student.
5. Design an entry form. Include a place for the student's name, project title, hypothesis, method, materials, and student and parent signatures.
6. Compile a list of suggested science fair topics.
7. Draft a cover letter (to be signed by the principal) which introduces the fair and explains the rules.
8. Design an evaluation form.
9. Secure judges.
10. Send each judge a judging packet which includes the fair rules, the judging criteria, and a list of the projects to be judged.
11. Order or prepare certificates.
12. Plan and type the science fair program.
13. Plan the science fair layout and gather all of the necessary materials and equipment such as tables, chairs, a portable address system, etc.
14. Send thank-yous to parent and teacher volunteers, judges, and demonstrators after the science fair.

STUDENT CHECKLIST FOR SCIENCE FAIR PROJECTS

1. Does the project deal with a specific problem?
2. Can the question be answered through a scientific investigation?
3. Do you have a set of expectations for this investigation?
4. Have you stated your expectations before beginning the actual testing?
5. Do you have a materials and/or equipment list?
6. Could someone else set up and conduct your investigation from your step-by-step directions?
7. Have you taken pictures, made sketches, and/or kept a log?
8. Have you determined a table, chart or graph format?
9. Do you have a plan for accurately and creatively displaying your investigation procedure and results?

TWO DOZEN SCIENCE FAIR TOPICS

1. Do metals rust at different rates?
2. Which type of water evaporates the quickest: salt, tap, or fresh?
3. How are insects both harmful and helpful to human beings?
4. Does the time of day affect body temperature?
5. What forces change rocks to affect the earth's surface?
6. Which fruits contain a large quantity of acid?
7. Does color have an effect on a person's food choice? How?
8. How quickly can a mouse learn to run a maze?
9. What effect does loud noise have on growing plants?
10. How does air pollution affect plant and animal life?
11. Does magnetism affect an animal's behavior? How?
12. Does magnetism affect plant growth? How?
13. How do animals adapt to changing weather conditions?
14. Which packaging method best reduces the growth of mold or fungus?
15. Through what surfaces does sound travel best?
16. At what time during the day does the sun give the most energy?
17. What effect does the amount of sunlight have on the color of a leaf?
18. Does gravity affect the direction that a seed grows?
19. Does the brightness of a light have an effect on the amount of heat the light produces?
20. Does a thin liquid boil faster than a thick liquid?
21. Does caffeine affect plant growth? How?
22. What surfaces reflect light best?
23. What is the highest temperature at which milk may be stored and not spoil?
24. How much salt will a plant be able to tolerate and still grow?

CRITERIA FOR JUDGING SCIENCE FAIR PROJECTS

1. **Scientific Investigations** - *40 points*
   - Is the purpose stated on the display?
   - Is the procedure used in developing and obtaining the solution or results explained?

2. **Creative Ability** - *15 points*
   - Did the student design and construct any equipment?
   - Does this project display originality and creativity?
   - Is the data presented uniquely?

3. **Thoroughness** - *20 points*
   - Does the display physically demonstrate the operation or results?
   - Are accurate amounts of materials listed?

4. **Skill** - *15 points*
   - Is the demonstrated skill commensurate with the student's age and grade level?

5. **Clarity/Neatness** - *10 points*
   - Is the written material clearly presented?
   - Is the display well-organized and attractive?
   - Is the material readable and arranged in a logical manner?

GLOSSARY

ADAPTATION - change in behavior or form that helps an animal adjust to its environment

ANTENNA - either of a pair of long, thin feelers on the head of an insect

CALCIUM - a soft, white metal needed to grow strong, healthy bones which is found in limestone, chalk, milk, marble, etc.

CAMOUFLAGE - a disguise or false appearance that is used to hide something

CHROMA - refers to lightness or brightness of a given color

CIRCUMFERENCE - the boundary line of a circle

CLIMATE - the general weather conditions of a place or region which includes the average temperature, rainfall, humidity and wind conditions

CONCAVE - curving inward (the ends are thicker than the middle)

CONVEX - curving outward (the ends are thinner than the middle)

CRYSTAL - a piece of a mineral with a definite shape

DIAMETER - a straight line passing through the center of a circle and terminating at the outermost boundary

ENVIRONMENT - all the surrounding objects, conditions and influences that have to do with the development of living things

EXTINCT - no longer in existence

FORECAST - to predict the weather

HABITAT - the place where an animal or plant naturally lives and grows

HOMOGENEOUS - uniform in composition throughout

HUE - a particular tint or shade of a color

INORGANIC - not of living things or the products of living things

LARVA - the free-living form of an insect as it hatches from an egg

MAGNETIC FIELD - the power of magnetism around a magnet

MAGNETIC FORCE - a push or pull that affects objects near a magnet

METAMORPHOSIS - a series of changes in shape, structure or function that certain animals go through as they develop into an adult

MINERAL - a homogeneous inorganic substance which has a definite chemical composition and specific crystalline structure, color and hardness

NATURE - the physical universe (all things that are not made by humans)

PALEONTOLOGIST - one who studies fossils

PERISCOPE - an instrument consisting of a tube containing lenses & mirrors which is used to see objects reflected at the other end of the eyepiece (such as on a submarine)

PITCH - the highness or lowness of a sound

POLES - the two ends of a magnet having the strongest force

PREDICTION - using given information to guess or tell what will happen beforehand

PREHISTORIC - belonging to a time before recorded history

PREY - an animal that is hunted or seized for food

PRIMARY COLORS - the three basic colors (red, yellow, blue) from which all other colors can be made

PUPA - the stage of an insect between the larva and adult stages

SECONDARY COLORS - all colors formed by the various combinations of the primary colors

SEED - the part of a plant from which a new plant will grow

SENSES - the five faculties of receiving impressions through body organs and the nerves associated with them (sight, taste, touch, smell and hearing)

SKELETON - the framework of bones of a vertebrate animal body that supports the tissues and protects the organs

SPECIES - a group of animals or plants that have certain common characteristics

UNICYCLE - a vehicle similar to a bicycle which has only one wheel

VIBRATION - a rapid movement back and forth

VITAMINS - substances that are needed in small amounts for the health and the normal functioning of the body

pg. 28

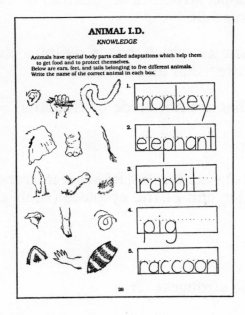

pg. 31 Bobcat: sharp claws, teeth, speed
Deer: speed, sight, smell, hearing
Rabbit: sight, speed, hearing, hind legs
Raccoon: claws
Squirrel: speed, claws
Bird: flight
Porcupine: sharp spines
Badger: sharp claws, teeth

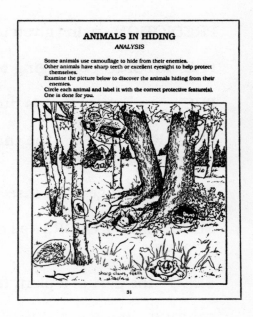

pg. 38

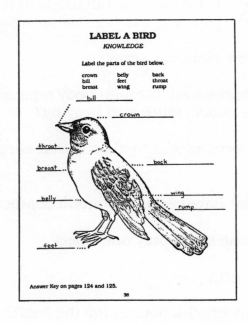

pg. 41 A. 1)A 2)B 3)D 4)C 5)F 6)E 7)H 8)G 9)I 10)J

BIRDS WORTH REMEMBERING
JUST FOR FUN

Look carefully at this picture for three minutes.
Then cover the picture with a clean sheet of paper and write the names of as many birds as you can remember on the paper.

DINOSAUR DECISIONS
KNOWLEDGE

Match the picture of each dinosaur with the correct description by writing the correct letter in each blank.
Color the dinosaurs.

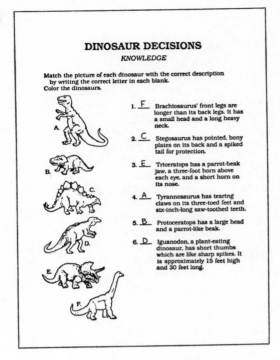

1. **F** Brachiosaurus' front legs are longer than its back legs. It has a small head and a long heavy neck.

2. **C** Stegosaurus has pointed, bony plates on its back and a spiked tail for protection.

3. **E** Triceratops has a parrot-beak jaw, a three-foot horn above each eye, and a short horn on its nose.

4. **A** Tyrannosaurus has tearing claws on its three-toed feet and six-inch-long saw-toothed teeth.

5. **B** Protoceratops has a large head and a parrot-like beak.

6. **D** Iguanodon, a plant-eating dinosaur, has short thumbs which are like sharp spikes. It is approximately 15 feet high and 30 feet long.

DINOSAUR DOT-TO-DOT
JUST FOR FUN

Tyrannosaurus is believed to have been the largest, most powerful flesh-eating creature to ever walk the earth.
Tyrannosaurus weighed more than seven tons and had a body nearly fifty feet long.

Standing on two huge back legs, Tyrannosaurus ripped flesh from its unfortunate victims with sharp teeth and tearing claws.
Connect the dots from A to Z to uncover a picture of this most feared of all dinosaurs!

LEGS, LEGS, LEGS
KNOWLEDGE

Every insect has six legs.
Circle each picture below of a critter that is not an insect.
Color the insects.

  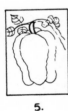

1.   2.   3.   4.   5.   6.

pg. 69 flower-cauliflower; seed-corn; fruit-apple; stem-celery; leaf-lettuce; root-carrot

INDEX